Roald Dahl
The Storyteller

Jason Hook

Raintree

Chicago, Illinois

Titles in this series:
Muhammad Ali: The Greatest—Neil Armstrong: The First Man on the Moon—Fidel Castro: Leader of Cuba's Revolution—The Dalai Lama: Peacemaker from Tibet—Anne Frank: Voice of Hope—Mahatma Gandhi: The Peaceful Revolutionary—Bill Gates: Computer Legend—Martin Luther King, Jr.: Civil Rights Hero—John Lennon: Musician with a Message—Nelson Mandela: Father of Freedom—Wolfgang Amadeus Mozart: Musical Genius—Florence Nightingale: The Lady of the Lamp—Pope John Paul II: Pope for the People—Pablo Picasso: Master of Modern Art—Elvis Presley: The King of Rock and Roll—Queen Elizabeth II: Monarch of Our Times—The Queen Mother: Grandmother of a Nation—William Shakespeare: Poet and Playwright—Vincent Van Gogh: The Troubled Artist

© 2004 Raintree
Published by Raintree, a division of Reed Elsevier, Inc.
Chicago, Illinois
Customer Service 888-363-4266
Visit our website at www.raintreelibrary.com

Raintree
100 N. LaSalle, Suite 1200
Chicago, IL 60602

Library of Congress Cataloging-in-Publication Data:
Hook, Jason.
  Roald Dahl / Jason Hook.
    p. cm. -- (Famous lives)
Summary: Introduces the life and work of children's author Roald Dahl, whose famous characters include Charlie, Willy Wonka, Matilda, James, and the BFG.
  ISBN 0-7398-6626-5 (Library Binding-hardcover)
  1. Dahl, Roald--Juvenile literature. 2. Authors, English--20th century--Biography--Juvenile literature. 3. Children's stories--Authorship--Juvenile literature. [1. Dahl, Roald--Juvenile literature. 2. Authors, English.] I. Title. II. Series: Famous lives (Chicago, Ill.)
  PR6054.A35Z69 2004
  823'.914--dc21
                    2003003675

Printed in Hong Kong

1 2 3 4 5 6 7 8 9 0 LB 07 06 05 04 03

Cover: Roald Dahl outside his writing shed.
Title page: Roald Dahl enjoyed writing horror and suspense stories.

Acknowledgments
The publishers would like to thank the Roald Dahl literary estate for their assistance with this book.

Picture acknowledgments
p. 4 Camera Press; p. 5 Pictorial Press; pp. 6 (top), 8, 10–11, 13, 14, 16, 34, 36, 40, 44 Roald Dahl literary estate; pp. 6–7 Patricia Aithie/Ffotograph; pp. 9, 10 (top), 12 Mary Evans; pp. 15, 19, 21, 22, 26, 32 Popperfoto; pp. 17, 23 Corbis; p. 18 Hodder Wayland Picture Library; pp. 20, 31, 33, 38, 39 Topham; pp. 24, 28, 32 Rex; p. 25 © Guild/Disney/Allied filmmakers/Pictorial Press; p27 Rex/LmcCombe/TPX; p. 29 © David Wolper/Pictorial Press, pp. 30, 35 © Portobello Productions/Pictorial Press; pp. 37, 45 Richard Stonehouse/Camera Press; p. 41 © Warner/Lorimar/Pictorial Press; p. 43 © Columbia Tristar/Jersey/Pictorial Press.

Cover photo: Roald Dahl Literary Estate
Title page photo: Popperfoto

Contents

The Inventing Room

Hidden away in a tool shed, a giant man sits writing. His feet are propped against a battered suitcase, a blanket covers his legs, and on his lap rests the wooden board on which he works. A hole is cut in the back of his ancient armchair to stop it from pressing against his aching spine.

"*On the door it said, INVENTING ROOM—PRIVATE—KEEP OUT. Mr. Wonka took a key from his pocket, leaned over the side of the boat, and put the key in the keyhole. 'This is the most important room in the entire factory!' he said. 'All my most secret new inventions are cooking and simmering in here!'*"
Roald Dahl, *Charlie and the Chocolate Factory* (1964).

Roald Dahl in the tool shed where he invented his characters.

Willy Wonka and the children from the 1971 movie **Willy Wonka and the Chocolate Factory.** *From left to right: Augustus Gloop, Violet Beauregarde, Charlie Bucket (standing in front of Willy Wonka), Veruca Salt, and Mike Tevee.*

Scattered over a writing desk beside him is a collection of strange objects. Each offers a clue to the life he has led and the stories he has written. There is a heavy silver ball, made entirely of chocolate wrappers; a carved grasshopper; his father's knife; a **valve** used in children's brain surgery; a model of a Hurricane fighter plane; and a large bone, removed from his own hip.

These objects must weave a certain magic. For the writer is Roald Dahl, and it is in this hideaway that he invents his famous characters: James, Willy Wonka, Matilda, and the BFG.

My Father

Roald Dahl lived an unusual life, so it is perhaps not surprising that his story starts even before he was born! His father, Harald Dahl, believed that his son would grow up to love beautiful things if he experienced them from inside the womb. So Harald insisted on taking his pregnant wife, Sofie, on "glorious walks" through the beautiful countryside.

Harald was Norwegian but had made his fortune as a **shipbroker** in Wales. He was a determined man who had overcome many problems to achieve his success.

Harald and Sofie Dahl, Roald's parents, on their wedding day.

> *"When I was a boy, I was an avid collector of birds' eggs.... To open a drawer and see thirty different very beautiful eggs nestling in their compartments on pink cotton wool was a lovely sight."*
> Roald Dahl, *My Year* (1983).

The church in Cardiff Bay, Llandaff, Wales, where Roald Dahl was christened.

When he was fourteen, his left arm had been **amputated** after an accident. In 1907 his first wife died, leaving him with two children.

Harald remarried after meeting Sofie Hesselberg on a trip home to Norway. With Sofie, Harald had four more children. Roald, their only boy, was born on September 13, 1916, in Llandaff in Wales. The glorious walks seem to have worked—he would grow up to love collecting beautiful objects, from birds' eggs and roses to **antiques** and paintings.

Boy

Both Roald and his father would suffer from tragedies throughout their lives. When Roald was three, and while his mother was pregnant again, his seven-year-old sister, Astri, died from **appendicitis.** Two months later his grieving father died from **pneumonia.** Years later the heroes of many of Roald Dahl's stories would be **orphans,** or children with a single parent.

Roald on vacation with his family in Norway.

When Roald was a young boy his mother told him folktales about Norwegian giants like the one illustrated here.

"My grandmother was Norwegian. The Norwegians know all about witches, for Norway, with its black forests and icy mountains, is where the first witches came from."
Roald Dahl, *The Witches* (1983).

Left a widow in a foreign country, Sofie moved into a smaller house and raised six children. Despite the family's misfortunes, Roald's childhood was far from unhappy. He adored his mother, remembering: "Her children **radiated** round her like planets round a sun."

Every summer Sofie took the whole family on vacation to Norway. These were magical journeys for Roald, who listened wide-eyed to folktales about witches and giants that he would never forget. He kept a secret diary of his childhood adventures. But even as a child he needed a hideaway in which to write—a treehouse at the top of a horse chestnut tree.

The Chocolate Room

A 1929 advertisement for Cadbury's chocolate.

At the age of nine, Roald was sent off to **boarding school.** He went first to St. Peter's, and then to Repton, a "public school" (what the British call a private school), both in England. Tall for his age, he was outstanding at sports. He was also an eager photographer and found a new hideaway in the school darkroom. But Roald showed little promise in English or his other classes.

At Repton teachers and older boys terrorized younger students with whippings and vicious bullying. Dahl never got over this, and the theme of taking revenge on bullies would play a part in many of his stories.

> "And it wasn't simply an ordinary enormous chocolate factory, either. It was the largest and most famous in the whole world! It was WONKA'S FACTORY, owned by a man called Mr. Willy Wonka, the greatest inventor and maker of chocolates that there has ever been."
>
> Roald Dahl, *Charlie and the Chocolate Factory* (1964).

Repton also provided Roald with a happier theme—chocolate! Cadbury's (the British chocolate manufacturer) sent their latest inventions to the school, so that students could rate them. Roald Dahl's lifelong love of chocolate began, and he dreamed of becoming an inventor for Cadbury's. Instead he would one day write a story about the greatest chocolate inventor of them all.

Roald's first boarding school, St. Peter's.

It's Off to Work We Go!

During his last semester at Repton, Roald secretly kept a motorcycle on which he could roar around the countryside. He said: "It gave me an amazing feeling of winged **majesty** and of independence."

A desire for even greater independence prompted him to accept a job with the Shell Oil Company. At first he was stuck behind a desk in London, where he built the ball of chocolate wrappers that would one day be kept in his writing shed. But he longed to sail to "distant and magic lands."

A 1929 advertisement for the Shell Oil Company.

In 1938, 22-year-old Roald Dahl was sent on a three-year job to Dar es Salaam, Tanzania, on the eastern coast of Africa. Here he found the adventures he craved. He learned to speak Swahili, visited diamond mines, and rescued a servant from a deadly black mamba snake. He also sold his first article, telling the true story of a local cook's wife who was rescued unharmed from a lion's jaws.

"Oh, lion dear, could I not make
You happy with a lovely steak
Could I entice you from your lair
With rabbit pie or roasted hare?
The lion smiled and shook his head.
He came up very close and said,
'The meat I am about to chew
Is neither steak nor chops.
IT'S YOU.'"
Roald Dahl, "The Lion," from *Dirty Beasts* (1983).

Dahl, age 22, in Dar es Salaam, where he had his first great adventures.

13

Going Solo

Dahl, in Nairobi at the start of World War II.

When World War II broke out in 1939, Dahl seized the opportunity for even greater adventure. He drove his battered old car 620 miles (1,000 kilometers) to Nairobi, Kenya, and **enlisted** in the Royal Air Force (RAF).

"Oh, it was wonderful to be flying on the back of this great swan! It was wonderful to be up in the air and to feel the air swishing past his face."
Roald Dahl, *The Minpins* (1991).

Training to be a pilot was the happiest time of Dahl's life. He never forgot the joy of soaring through the air while watching herds of wild animals sweeping over the plain beneath him. Many of his children's stories would include amazing flights. He was so tall, his head stuck up out of the cockpit, causing the other pilots to nickname him "Lofty."

An RAF plane in Egypt during World War II.

On September 19, 1940, with his training complete, Dahl was ordered to fly to an airfield in Egypt to join his squadron. He got lost and, running short of fuel, he crash-landed in the desert. His head lurched forward into the plane's gun-sight, driving his nose back into his skull. Blinded and bleeding, Roald somehow dragged himself to safety. Moments later his plane burst into flames.

The Author

Dahl in a tented camp in Greece in 1941.

> **"I remember looking down the nose of the machine at the ground ... and my stomach felt as though someone were using it as a pincushion for rusty hatpins."**
> Roald Dahl, "Shot Down over Libya" (1942).

Despite spending six months in the hospital to recover from his injuries, Dahl refused to be sent home. He finally joined up with his squadron in Greece and went on to successfully shoot down at least five enemy planes in combat. But in the summer of 1941, severe headaches forced him to return to England.

A golden opportunity now came Dahl's way. Believing that this tall, talkative flying ace might help to attract American support of the war, the Air Ministry sent him across the Atlantic to Washington, D.C., as a **diplomat.**

The British writer C. S. Forester, who was famous for writing stories about a naval officer named Horatio Hornblower.

In Washington Dahl had a lucky meeting with a famous author named C. S. Forester, who, wanting to write about fighter pilots during the war, asked Dahl to provide some notes. Instead Dahl wrote a complete story, a thrilling mix of fact and fiction. The *Saturday Evening Post* immediately published it under the title "Shot Down over Libya." Dahl received a check for $900, and Forester asked him, "Did you know you were a writer?" His new career had begun.

Adventure

The next part of Roald Dahl's life sounds like something from one of his stories. Britain recruited him to spy on the most powerful people in Washington. Dahl was soon mixing with other writers who were also interested in the war, including Ian Fleming, the author of *Chitty Chitty Bang Bang* and the creator of James Bond.

Hollywood actress Ava Gardner with the writer Ernest Hemingway, whom Dahl met in Washington.

To meet the rich and famous, Dahl used his talents as a storyteller. He had continued to write short stories about the war, and he would recite these at dinner parties. One of his tales, *The Gremlins* (1943), was his first children's story. It was based on a popular Royal Air Force myth about little creatures causing mechanical problems on aircrafts. It found its way onto the desk of Walt Disney, and, at the age of 25, Dahl was invited to Hollywood.

"He saw a little man, scarcely more than six inches high, with a large round face and a little pair of horns growing out of his head. On his legs were a pair of shiny black suction boots, which made it possible for him to remain standing on the wing at 300 miles an hour."
Roald Dahl, *The Gremlins* (1943).

Plans for a film were canceled, but Disney published the story. Eleanor Roosevelt, the wife of President Franklin D. Roosevelt, loved the story, and Dahl found himself having dinner at the White House!

Five people had to operate the camera used to photograph cartoons in the Walt Disney Studios in Hollywood in the 1940s.

Lamb to the Slaughter

When the war ended in 1945, Dahl returned to England to live with his mother in the rural village of Great Missenden, Buckinghamshire. Dahl enjoyed country life, and he spent time with the local men who enjoyed hunting. He still loved to collect beautiful things and made a living buying paintings and **antiques** for his new wealthy friends in the United States.

All the while Dahl was writing. In 1946 a collection of his war stories, *Over to You*, received excellent reviews. He then wrote one of the first novels about nuclear war, *Sometime Never* (1948), but the book was not popular.

Dahl had also started inventing strange, dark tales with unexpected twists at the end. In "Lamb to the Slaughter" (1953), a woman kills her husband with a frozen leg of lamb, then cooks the murder weapon and serves it to detectives. In "Skin" (1952), a man sells a picture by a famous artist even though it is tattooed on his back. Such sinister plots would bring Dahl the fame he craved.

Great Missenden, Buckinghamshire, where Dahl lived with his mother after World War II.

"*It wasn't nasty. I thought it was hilarious. What's horrible is basically funny. In fiction.*" Roald Dahl talking about "Lamb to the Slaughter" (1953).

Dahl's fascination with horror would influence his adult and children's stories.

Someone Like You

At the age of 35, Dahl accepted a friend's invitation to move to New York City. There, at exactly 6:45 P.M. on October 20, 1952, he found himself at a dinner party seated beside the famous Hollywood actress Patricia Neal. We know the time because Dahl would later frame the page from his calendar.

The bright lights of New York City, where Dahl met Patricia Neal in 1952. At first Neal disliked Dahl, but she soon grew to love him.

"I tried to join the conversation but he totally ignored me. I was infuriated and tried to pretend his rudeness did not bother me in the least, but by the end of the evening, I had made up my mind that I loathed [hated] Roald Dahl." Patricia Neal recalls her first meeting with Roald Dahl in her autobiography *As I Am* (1988).

Dahl and his wife Patricia Neal, a year after they married.

The following July they were married. The happy couple rented an apartment in New York and bought a home in Great Missenden near Dahl's family, which they called Gipsy House. It was at Gipsy House that Dahl would create his latest hideaway: the tool shed where he worked. Dahl honeymooned in Europe with his glamorous wife and returned to New York just as a collection of his short stories was published. Titled _Someone Like You,_ the book was a huge success.

The Giant Peach

Patricia Neal and Roald Dahl had their first child, Olivia, in 1955. A daughter, Tessa, came in 1957, followed by a son, Theo, in 1960.

Dahl had used his skills as a storyteller to enter Washington society. Now he used them to step into his children's world. Each night he amazed them with marvelous, magical tales. Their favorite was about an **orphan**, James, who escapes his bullying aunts by flying away in a giant peach full of friendly insects.

Roald Dahl and Patricia Neal at Gipsy House with their children: Olivia, Tessa, and baby Theo.

In 1960 a second collection of Dahl's sinister adult tales, *Kiss, Kiss,* was published. His fame was growing, but Dahl was running short of ideas, and so he sent his publishers a children's story instead. *James and the Giant Peach* came out the following year. The story mixed elements of traditional fairy tales, **black humor,** and comic poems, and children loved it.

James and his insect friends, in the 1997 Disney movie version of Dahl's story James and the Giant Peach.

"The peach rolled on. And behind it, Aunt Sponge and Aunt Spiker lay ironed out upon the grass as flat and thin and lifeless as a couple of paper dolls cut out of a picture book."
Roald Dahl, *James and the Giant Peach* (1961).

Family Life

Roald Dahl's life, like his father's, was an extraordinary mix of success and terrible trouble. In the winter of 1960, the Dahls' nanny was pushing Theo's stroller across a New York street when it was struck by a taxi. The impact shattered the four-month-old baby's skull.

Patricia Neal with her children during Theo's long recovery from his accident.

Roald Dahl with engineer and friend, Stanley Wade. They were a major part of the team that invented the Wade-Dahl-Till valve.

"He fought misfortune as if it was a dragon to be slain."
The *Guardian*, 1996.

Somehow Theo survived. But fluid built up around his brain and a drainage tube had to be inserted into his head. A **valve** in this type of tube frequently became blocked, causing infection, and Theo had to have a series of dangerous operations.

Dahl always believed that when anything went wrong he could make things better. He moved his family to Gipsy House permanently and began working on the problem of the valve himself. Together with Stanley Wade, an engineer with whom he had once flown model airplanes, and Kenneth Till, a surgeon, he invented the Wade-Dahl-Till valve. By some miracle Theo recovered without the valve. But it would be used to help thousands of injured children in the future.

The Chocolate Factory

As Theo recovered, a light was wired up in the writing shed so that Patricia could signal to her husband in emergencies. Dahl was always a slow, **painstaking** writer, and it was a struggle before he finished his next book: *Charlie and the Chocolate Factory* (1964).

"What distinguished Roald most of all is that he was, quite simply, a magician. Those who were lucky enough to get to know him experienced his magic powers directly. And for others, perhaps Roald became a writer so that he could cast his spells by telling them stories."
Dahl's publisher, Tom Maschler, "On Publishing Roald Dahl" (1997).

Dahl in his writing shed at Gipsy House, deep in thought.

A scene from the 1971 movie Willy Wonka and the Chocolate Factory.

Dedicated to Theo, *Charlie and the Chocolate Factory* tells of a group of children who win golden tickets to visit Willy Wonka's chocolate factory. Here tiny workers called Oompa-Loompas produce magical candies. Four of the children are led by their own greed to terrible fates. But Charlie, the hero, inherits the factory. Willy Wonka is in many ways like his author. Rude and childlike, he demands that everyone play by his rules; but he is also a magician who creates wonders.

Some **critics** praised the humor of Dahl's latest book. Others said it was tasteless. But children loved it. By 1968, in the United States alone, *Charlie and the Chocolate Factory* had sold over half a million copies.

November

As much as Dahl's career was blessed, his personal life seemed filled with sadness. On November 17, 1962, as Theo was recovering, the Dahls' eldest daughter, Olivia, died suddenly after catching measles. She was seven, the same age Roald's sister Astri had been when she died. Roald's grief nearly destroyed him.

The Dahls continued on. Roald, the lover of beauty, collected hundreds of miniature plants and built a rock garden in memory of his daughter. Patricia made the film *Hud* (1963), which would win her an Academy Award (Oscar). Then in 1964 the Dahls had a new daughter, Ophelia.

Patricia Neal and Paul Newman, two of Hollywood's most glamorous stars, in the 1963 movie **Hud.**

> *"Some people, when they ... have been driven beyond the point of endurance, simply crumble and give up. There are others, though they are not many, who will for some reason always be unconquerable. They have an indomitable [very strong] spirit, and nothing ... will cause them to give up."*
> Roald Dahl, "The Swan," from *The Wonderful Story of Henry Sugar and Six More* (1977).

But there was more tragedy ahead. In 1965 Patricia, who was pregnant again and working in Hollywood, suffered three **strokes.** She was left crippled, blind in one eye, and unable to speak. Then on November 17, 1967, Roald's mother, Sofie, died. It was five years, to the day, since the death of Olivia.

Wearing an eyepatch and a brace on her leg, Patricia Neal returns to England to begin her long, slow recovery.

31

The Second Miracle

The Dahl family at home after Patricia's strokes.

"As I am telling you before, I know exactly what words I am wanting to say, but somehow or other they is always getting squiff-squiddled around."
Roald Dahl, *The BFG* (1982).

After her **strokes** Patricia had to learn to speak all over again. Her words came out muddled: a "spoonful of sugar" became a "soap driver;" a "cigarette" was an "oblogong." Dahl would later remember these when he wrote about a tongue-twisted giant in *The BFG* (1982).

Back at Gipsy House, Dahl organized a group of family and friends to give Patricia hours of tutoring each day. He also forced her to make speeches at public events. Some people were horrified by the way Dahl bullied his wife, but Dahl believed this was the only way she would make a full recovery. And recover she did. Their daughter, Lucy, was born in August 1965, and Patricia soon returned to acting.

Meanwhile, Dahl wrote two film scripts based on novels by his old friend Ian Fleming. One was the James Bond adventure *You Only Live Twice*. The other was *Chitty Chitty Bang Bang,* which had some familiar characters: a hero who invents candy, and a villain who can smell children!

The 2002 stage show of Chitty Chitty Bang Bang *in London. Dahl wrote the script for the movie version.*

The Champion of the World

At Gipsy House Roald Dahl had created a magical world for his children. In the yard there were a hundred different roses, brightly colored Australian parrots, a maze, and an old gypsy (Romany) **caravan**.

The caravan at Dahl's home, which also appears in **Danny the Champion of the World** *(1975).*

During Patricia's recovery Roald worked tirelessly to keep this dreamworld alive. He drove his children to school still wearing his pajamas and slippers. From the ceiling of the children's bedroom, he hung 50 colored glass balls and told them the reflections would scare off witches.

Dahl's next major book, *Danny the Champion of the World* (1975), features the type of magical father that Dahl hoped to be. Danny has no mother, but lives in a gypsy caravan with his father. The father tells Danny wonderful stories, makes him kites and hot-air balloons, and teaches him to drive a car at a young age—all things that Dahl did with his own children. Together Danny and his father defeat a bullying landowner by **poaching** his pheasants. The story is all about Dahl's belief that a parent should be "sparky," not boring.

"It was impossible to be bored in my father's company. He was too sparky a man for that. Plots and plans and new ideas came flying off him like sparks from a grindstone." Roald Dahl, *Danny the Champion of the World* (1975).

My Father's Deep Dark Secret

As he entered his sixties, Dahl suffered increasing pain from his wartime injuries. After having a hip replacement, he placed the old bone on his writing desk.

Dahl in his sixties, enjoying fame and success.

"No father is perfect. Grown-ups are complicated creatures, full of quirks [odd habits] and secrets. Some have quirkier quirks and deeper secrets than others, but all of them, including one's own parents, have two or three private habits hidden up their sleeves that would probably make you gasp if you knew about them."
Roald Dahl, *Danny the Champion of the World* (1975).

His success continued. In 1979 Dahl's adult stories were turned into the television series *Tales of the Unexpected,* in which Dahl appeared as a sinister storyteller. Meanwhile, the artist Quentin Blake began working on Dahl's children's stories. His mischievous and funny drawings reflect the humor shown in Dahl's writing and were the perfect illustrations for new works such as *The Enormous Crocodile* (1978), *The Twits* (1980), and *Revolting Rhymes* (1982).

Things were also changing at home. For several years Dahl had been keeping a secret. He was in love with Felicity Crossland, a friend of Patricia's. Eventually, Patricia left and Felicity moved into Gipsy House.

This 2001 stage play captures the wildness and gross humor of Dahl's story The Twits (1980).

Journey to a Dream Country

Dahl used to tell his children that their dreams were created by a big, friendly giant who blew magical powders through their bedroom window. He would then say goodnight and creep out into the yard. Climbing up a ladder, he would slide a bamboo cane through their window and gently blow!

A stage version of The BFG, *based on Dahl's novel, shown at a London theater in 2002.*

"When all the other giants is galloping off every what way and which to swollop human beans, I is scuddling away to other places to blow dreams into the bedrooms of sleeping children. Nice dreams. Lovely golden dreams. Dreams that is giving the dreamers a happy time."
Roald Dahl, *The BFG* (1983).

This idea led to *The BFG*, which featured one of Dahl's greatest characters. The dream-blowing BFG (Big Friendly Giant) speaks terrible English, or "wigglish." He drinks frobscottle, a delicious fizzy drink with sinking bubbles that cause him to "whizzpop." The BFG is bullied by even bigger giants until he is helped by a little **orphan**, whom Dahl named after Tessa's new daughter, Sophie.

At the end of the book, the BFG sneaks Sophie into the queen's bedroom at Buckingham Palace. Shortly after Dahl had finished the book, the royal bedroom really was broken into by an intruder—much to Dahl's amusement!

Dahl named the heroine of The BFG *after his granddaughter, Sophie, shown here with her mother, Tessa.*

The Grand High Witch

Dahl was happy. Gipsy House was filled with beautiful
paintings and **antiques** that Dahl had collected.
He enjoyed good food and still handed out chocolates
to his many visitors. And he was writing better than ever.
In 1983 he married Felicity.

Dahl also enjoyed what he called his "child power," saying if
he knocked on a child's door anywhere in the world he hoped
he might be invited in for a cup of tea. On more than one
occasion he arranged for **orphans** from Italy to visit Great
Missenden and share in the magic of Gipsy House. Dahl's
tales had been published everywhere from Australia to China,
and in 1983 *The Witches* won him the prestigious **Whitbread
Prize.** The judges said they were "in the hands of a master."

*Roald and Felicity on
their wedding day.*

"By then I'll be a very old mouse and you'll be a very old grandmother and soon after that we'll both die together."
Roald Dahl, *The Witches* (1983).

Angelica Huston plays the terrifying Grand High Witch in the 1989 movie version of Dahl's story, **The Witches.**

While writing *The Witches*, Dahl clearly thought about his own life. The story recalls childhood tales from Norway and features a witch-hunting grandmother Dahl based on his own mother. During the tale, the hero—again an orphan—is turned into a mouse. He is happy because he will live only as long as his beloved grandmother, thus avoiding the pain of loss that Dahl had suffered throughout his life.

The Third Miracle

Roald Dahl, age 73, outside the hut that was his "inventing room."

In his final years, Dahl became a very controversial figure. He made an outspoken attack on Israel, criticized the author Salman Rushdie, and turned down the title of Officer of the British Empire because he felt he deserved a knighthood. But then he had never been afraid of offending people, which is perhaps why children love his stories.

When Dahl was diagnosed with cancer, he vowed to fight it as he had fought misfortune all his life. He continued to hobble down to his writing hut and completed two autobiographies, *Boy* (1984) and *Going Solo* (1986). By some miracle, he also found the energy to continue writing children's stories. *Matilda* (1988), about a little girl who uses magical powers to defeat her bullying teacher, Miss Trunchbull, became his fastest-selling book.

He also had time to collect one last thing of beauty, bidding from his hospital bed for a painting by Vincent van Gogh. On November 23, 1990, at age 74, Roald Dahl died. November was the month that had always brought him tragedy.

"She felt as though she had touched something that was not quite of this world, the highest point of the heavens, the farthest star."
Roald Dahl, *Matilda* (1988).

*A movie version of **Maltida** was made in 1996.*

The Magic Finger

Like the inventor Willy Wonka and the dream-blowing BFG, Roald Dahl knew how to weave magic for children. That is why the characters he created in a tool shed live on today. They appear in films, plays, and concerts around the world, and Dahl's books have been translated into more than 30 languages. With money created by Roald's magical characters, Felicity set up the Roald Dahl Foundation to support charities for children.

Dahl's own children have now grown up, and they still cherish memories of their father's bedtime stories. His granddaughter Sophie inherited both his height and his desire to write. She became famous as a fashion model, and in 2002 she published a book called *The Man with the Dancing Eyes*.

A Dutch edition of The BFG. Dahl's books have been published in many different languages.

"If you want to remember what it's like to live in a child's world, you've got to get down on your hands and knees and live like that for a week. You'll find you have to look up at all these ... giants around you who are always telling you what to do and what not to do." Roald Dahl, *The Roald Dahl Guide to Railway Safety* (1991).

Some adults criticized the **black humor** of Roald Dahl's books. But he felt that they had simply forgotten what it was like to be a child. As he wrote in *The Minpins* (1991), which was published after his death: "Those who don't believe in magic will never find it."

Glossary

amputated cut off by a surgeon

antique item of furniture or other object that is valuable because of its age

appendicitis inflammation of an organ called the appendix. Today people rarely die from appendicitis.

avid enthusiastic, devoted

black humor humor that makes something sad or tragic seem funny

boarding school a place where students live full time

caravan a horse-drawn cart used for both transportation and shelter

critic person whose job it is to review new books, plays, and movies

diplomat somebody who represents their government in a foreign country

enlisted signed up to serve in the military

majesty dignity or beauty

orphan child whose parents have died

painstaking extremely careful

pneumonia serious infection of the lungs, which can sometimes lead to death

poaching hunting or catching animals and fish on somebody else's land

radiated spread out from a central point

shipbroker somebody who arranges supplies and passengers for ships

stroke attack caused by a change in the flow of blood to the brain, which can leave the victim with a serious disability

valve device that controls the flow of a fluid

Whitbread Prize major British prize for the writer of the year's best book

Further Information

Books to Read

Dahl, Roald. *Boy/Going Solo*. New York: Puffin, 2001.

Dahl, Roald. *The Roald Dahl Treasury*. New York: Viking, 1997.

Middleton, Haydn. *Roald Dahl*. Chicago: Heinemann, 1998.

Powling, Chris. *Roald Dahl: A Biography*. Minneapolis: Carolrhoda, 1994.

Shavick, Andrea. *Roald Dahl*. New York: Oxford University Press, 1998.

Date Chart

1911 Harald Dahl marries Sofie Hesselberg.

September 13, 1916 Roald Dahl is born in Llandaff, Wales.

1919 Roald's sister, Astri, dies from appendicitis.

1938 Sent to Africa by the Shell Oil Company

1939 Joins the RAF in Kenya.

1940 Crashes his airplane, experiencing what he calls a "monumental bash on the head"

1953 Marries Patricia Neal. They have five children: Olivia (1955), Tessa (1957), Theo (1960), Ophelia (1964), and Lucy (1965).

1960 Theo seriously injured in a street accident. Dahl invents the Wade-Dahl-Till valve.

1962 Olivia dies after catching measles.

1965 Patricia Dahl has three strokes. Dahl works on screenplay for *You Only Live Twice*.

1967 Dahl's mother, Sofie, dies.

1977 Has a hip replacement

1978 Begins working with Quentin Blake.

1979 Appears as a sinister storyteller in the TV series *Tales of the Unexpected*.

1983 Dahl and Patricia are divorced. Dahl marries Felicity Crossland. Wins the Whitbread Prize for *The Witches*.

November 23, 1990 Roald Dahl dies at age 74.

Works

1942: "Shot Down over Libya"

1943: *The Gremlins*

1946: *Over to You*

1948: *Sometime Never*

1953: *Someone Like You*. Adult short stories.

1960: *Kiss, Kiss*. More adult short stories.

1961: *James and the Giant Peach*

1964: *Charlie and the Chocolate Factory*

1966: *The Magic Finger*

1970: *Fantastic Mr. Fox*

1972: *Charlie and the Great Glass Elevator*

1975: *Danny the Champion of the World*

1977: *The Wonderful Story of Henry Sugar and Six More*. Short stories for children.

1978: *The Enormous Crocodile*

1979: *My Uncle Oswald*

1980: *The Twits*

1981: *George's Marvelous Medicine*

1982: *The BFG; Revolting Rhymes*

1983: *The Witches; Dirty Beasts*

1984: *Boy: Tales of Childhood*. First part of his autobiography.

1985: *The Giraffe and the Pelly and Me*

1986: *Going Solo*. Part two, autobiography.

1988: *Matilda*

1989: *Rhyme Stew*

1990: *Esio Trot*

1991: *The Vicar of Nibbleswicke, The Minpins,* and *My Year*

Index

All numbers in **bold** refer to pictures as well as text.